bake

bake

tina bester

PAVILION

contents

biscuits

cakes

meringues

sweet tarts and pastries

savoury tarts and old-fashioned pies

breads and buns

introduction

Bake consists of a series of easy-to-follow recipes, with mouthwatering images to inspire you to create easy-on-the-eye sweet and savoury feasts at home.

The book is divided into six sections and includes recipes for biscuits to fill up the cookie jar, savoury specialities such as the perfect roast chicken pie, an extensive selection of sweet tarts, cakes and meringue creations and essential recipes for fail-proof breads and buns.

The recipes and instructions included are tried-and-tested, uncomplicated and oh-so-easy to achieve, with snippets of no-nonsense advice from creator Tina Bester. *Bake* takes the fear factor out of this timeless tradition and celebrates the joy that a pretty iced cupcake, still-warm savoury tart or just-baked loaf of homemade bread can bring.

biscuits

double chocolate and pecan nut brownies

Decadent, rich and deliciously gooey, these are great served slightly warmed with chocolate sauce and a big dollop of whipped cream.

175g butter • 250g dark chocolate • 3 large eggs
250g castor sugar • 150g flour, sifted • 50g pecan nuts, chopped
200g dark chocolate, roughly chopped

Preheat the oven to 180°C. Line a 22cm square baking tin with wax paper.
Melt the butter and 250g of chocolate in a double boiler,
stirring until smooth, and then allow them to cool slightly.
Whisk together the eggs and sugar until light and fluffy,
then with the beaters still running pour the butter-and-chocolate
mixture into the eggs and sugar. Sift the flour and fold it into
the mixture. Add the nuts and extra 200g of chopped chocolate.
Pour into the tin and bake for 55 minutes.
Cool in the tin and cut into squares.

Makes 9

florentines

A hint of ginger in these chewy cookie-jar essentials adds zing.

100g butter, plus extra for greasing · 100g castor sugar
2 tablespoons preserved ginger in syrup, chopped
3 tablespoons sultanas (they are much better than raisins), chopped
120g flaked almonds · 100g dark chocolate, melted

Preheat the oven to 180°C. Melt the butter and sugar in
a pot and caramelize slightly (this will take about 5 minutes).
Combine the ginger with the sultanas and flaked almonds.
Add the butter and sugar mixture to the nut mixture and mix well.
Line a baking tray with baking paper, place 10 open-ended round metal
moulds on the tray and grease the insides of the ends with a little butter.
Divide the mixture evenly between the 10 moulds, pressing it
in with a spoon. Bake for 15 minutes. Allow them to cool and then
remove them from the moulds. Place the rounds on the baking
sheet and brush the underside of each one with melted chocolate.

Makes 10

hazelnut and chocolate cream biscuits

These biscuits have a wonderful macaroon-like
texture and are excellent with espresso.

100g hazelnuts ·250g icing sugar, plus extra for dusting
150g ground almonds · 1 large egg · 1 large egg yolk
chocolate cream · 250g dark chocolate, chopped · 100ml cream · 50g butter

Preheat the oven to 190°C. Roast the hazelnuts in a roasting pan for 8–10 minutes.
Allow them to cool slightly, place them in a clean dishcloth and rub them vigorously
to remove the skins. Grind them in a food processor until they are fairly fine.
Add the icing sugar and almonds and mix together. Add the egg and the egg yolk
and process to combine into a firm dough. Roll the dough into a sausage,
wrap it in clingwrap and place it in the fridge for 1 hour.

Increase the oven temperature to 200°C. Lightly sprinkle a work surface
with icing sugar and roll out the dough to 5mm thick. Cut out circles using a round
cookie cutter and lay them on a sheet of baking paper on a baking tray. Bake for
about 10 minutes until just golden brown and let them cool on the tray.

For the chocolate cream, place the chocolate, cream and butter in the top of a double
boiler and cook until the chocolate has melted and all the ingredients are combined.
Place the chocolate cream in the fridge, stirring from time to time, until it is thick
enough to spread between the biscuits. Spread a good dollop on the underside of half
the biscuits and sandwich together with the others. Dust lightly with icing sugar.

Makes 12 double biscuits

pat fraser's shortbread

Everyone should have this one in their arsenal of sure-fire
winning recipes — serve with a pot of strong tea.

200g flour · 200g butter
50g castor sugar, plus extra for dusting

Preheat the oven to 180°C.
Mix the flour and butter together in a food processor
and add the sugar. Process again until the mixture is crumbly.
Press into a greased fluted 22cm round tart tin with the back
of a spoon and bake for 30—35 minutes until golden brown.
(Be careful not to overcook it.) While the shortbread is still warm,
cut it into wedges, prick with a fork and dust with castor sugar.

Makes 8 wedges

caramel and chocolate shortbread

A dipping of dark chocolate brings a luxe element to these biscuits.

275g butter, softened · 160g castor sugar · 300g flour
150g cornflour · 300g dark chocolate, melted
caramel
1 x 385g tin condensed milk · 3 tablespoons golden syrup · 60g butter

Preheat the oven to 160˚C. To make the shortbread, cream the butter
and sugar together until pale and fluffy. Fold in the flour and cornflour
and roll into a 6cm-diameter sausage. Wrap it in clingwrap and refrigerate
for at least 1 hour. Slice the sausage into 4mm-thick slices and place
the slices on a lined baking sheet. Bake for 10–15 minutes.

To make the caramel, place the condensed milk, syrup
and butter in a pot and simmer gently for about 5 minutes,
stirring it all the time until the caramel thickens.

Now for the decadent part! Melt the chocolate, dip
each biscuit into the chocolate (covering half the biscuit)
and sandwich generously with the caramel.

Make 10 double biscuits

ginger and macadamia nut cookies

The ultimate milk and cookies recipe – dunk away!

50g butter · 60g castor sugar · 60g brown treacle sugar
1 large egg · 150g self-raising flour · 50g macadamia nuts, chopped
2 walnut-sized pieces glacé ginger, chopped
1 walnut-sized piece fresh ginger, finely grated

Preheat the oven to 180°C. Beat together the butter, sugars and egg.
Stir in the flour, nuts and ginger and mix together well.
Place tablespoons of the mixture onto a baking sheet lined
with baking paper and bake for 12–15 minutes.

Makes 10–12

jolly jammers

A sweet treat at any age — only strawberry jam will do for the filling!

200g butter · 100g icing sugar · 2 large egg yolks
1 teaspoon vanilla extract · 250g cake flour, plus extra for rolling
strawberry jam · icing sugar for dusting

Preheat the oven to 160°C. Beat the butter, icing sugar
and egg yolks together until thick and creamy, then add the
vanilla extract and flour and beat until the mixture forms a dough.
Wrap in clingfilm and place in the fridge for at least 1 hour.
Roll out the dough onto a lightly floured surface and cut out
16–20 rounds using a cookie cutter. Cut a heart shape out of the
centre of half of the rounds. Place them all on a tray lined with
baking paper and bake for 15–20 minutes until golden brown.
If they spread slightly and lose their shape, just re-cut them
as they come out of the oven, while the biscuits are still warm.
Allow to cool. To assemble, sandwich the whole rounds
and heart cut-out rounds together with strawberry jam.
Dust with icing sugar.

Makes 8–10 double biscuits

cakes

chocolate and almond cake
with chocolate ganache

A torte-like cake that's delicate yet utterly decadent.

250g dark chocolate · 250g butter · 100g castor sugar
4 large eggs · 100g self-raising flour, sifted · 80g ground almonds
chocolate ganache
400g dark chocolate, chopped · 250ml cream

Preheat the oven to 160°C. Line a 22cm spring-form cake tin
with baking paper. Melt the chocolate and butter together in a double boiler
and then allow the mixture to cool slightly. Beat the sugar and eggs together for
5 minutes until light and fluffy, then add the cooled chocolate-and-butter mixture
to the egg mixture, beating all the time. Fold in the flour and ground almonds.
Pour the mixture into the prepared tin and bake for 45–55 minutes until a tester
inserted into the cake comes out clean. The cake will feel very soft to the touch
and will crack around the edges, so don't be alarmed when this happens.

To make the ganache, melt the chocolate and cream together in a double boiler
and then place the mixture in the fridge to cool, stirring it from time to time.
Spread over the cooled cake just before serving.

Serves 8

mini carrot cakes with
lemon cream cheese icing

A must-have teatime treat, with a perfectly balanced sweet lemony icing.

175g brown sugar · 250ml vegetable oil · 4 large eggs · 200g cake flour
2 teaspoons baking powder · 1 teaspoon bicarbonate of soda
1 teaspoon cinnamon · 1 teaspoon ground ginger
250g grated carrot · 50g chopped pecan nuts, plus extra for decoration
80g sultanas · 125ml crushed pineapple
lemon cream cheese icing
60g butter · 250g icing sugar · 1 teaspoon vanilla extract
80g smooth cream cheese · grated zest of 1 lemon

Preheat the oven to 190°C. Lightly grease 20 mini loaf tins (5cm x 10cm)
and place them on a baking tray. Beat the sugar, oil and eggs together for 5 minutes
until fluffy. Sift the dry ingredients together and add to the sugar mixture together with
the grated carrot, nuts, sultanas and pineapple. Mix together well and pour into the
mini loaf tins. Bake for 30 minutes, turning them halfway through the baking time.

(To make a round 22cm cake, add an extra 100g of grated carrot and bake for about
1 hour and 15 minutes or until a tester inserted into the cake comes out clean.)

To make the icing, place all the ingredients in a mixing bowl and beat together until the
icing is light and fluffy. Ice the cooled cakes and decorate with the extra pecan nuts.

Makes 20 mini cakes

chocolate-dipped meringue-frosted chocolate cupcakes

The name's a mouthful and so are they — a chocolate extravaganza.

375g butter · 350g brown sugar · 3 large eggs · 250g flour, sifted
2 teaspoons baking powder · 50g cocoa · 180ml milk
meringue frosting
2 large egg whites · 175g castor sugar · 2 heaped tablespoons liquid glucose
(available at speciality baking stores) · 3 tablespoons water
pinch of cream of tartar · 300g dark chocolate

Preheat the oven to 190°C. Line 20 muffin cups with cupcake holders.
In a mixing bowl, beat the butter and sugar together for 10 minutes until light
and fluffy. Add the eggs, one at a time, beating well in between each addition.
Sift the dry ingredients together, fold them into the mixture and then stir in
the milk. Spoon the mixture into the cupcake holders and bake for 24 minutes,
turning the muffin tray halfway through the baking time. Allow to cool.

To make the meringue frosting, combine all the ingredients in a double boiler and
cook over a low heat, beating the mixture all the time with electric beaters until it
forms soft peaks. This will take about 7 minutes, but be careful not to overcook it.
Place the icing in a piping bag with a 1cm round nozzle and pipe spirals of the frosting
onto the tops of the cooled cupcakes. Place them in the fridge for 30 minutes and
in the meantime, melt the chocolate in a double boiler and allow it to cool slightly.
Dip each cupcake into the melted chocolate and allow the chocolate to set before serving.

Makes 20

chocolate and orange tea cakes

The tea-cup presentation adds an extra pretty element
(make sure to use oven-proof cups).

1 quantity chocolate cupcake recipe
(see chocolate-dipped meringue-frosted cupcakes recipe)
grated zest of 2 oranges
chocolate butter icing
110g butter, at room temperature
200g icing sugar, sifted
40g cocoa powder, sifted · 2 large eggs
1 teaspoon vanilla extract

Follow the method for the chocolate cupcakes, adding the orange
zest at the end (with the milk). To make the icing, beat the butter,
icing sugar and cocoa powder together and then add the eggs, one at a time.
Add the vanilla extract and beat again for a few minutes until it thickens
and becomes slightly fluffy. Use to ice the cooled cupcakes.

Makes 15–20

vanilla fairy cakes

The perfect canvas for fulfilling any cake-decorating desires.

250g butter, softened • 250g castor sugar • 4 large eggs
250g self-raising flour • I teaspoon vanilla extract
butter icing
800g icing sugar, sifted • 250g butter, softened • I large egg white
I teaspoon vanilla extract • I tablespoon ice water
royal icing
I large egg white • 200g icing sugar, sifted
300g–400g sugar-paste icing (available from speciality baking stores
and some supermarkets) • colour gels (available from speciality
baking stores and some supermarkets) • cornflour for dusting

Preheat the oven to 180°C. Line 36 muffin cups with cupcake holders of three
different sizes, 3cm, 5cm and 7cm (use 12 of each size). Beat the softened butter
and castor sugar until light and fluffy. Beat in the eggs one at a time. Fold in the
flour and the vanilla extract. Spoon the mixture into the cupcake holders and bake
the 3cm ones for 10 minutes, the 5cm ones for 16 minutes and the 7cm ones for
20 minutes, rotating each of the pans halfway through the baking times.

To make the butter icing, place the icing sugar, butter, egg white and vanilla extract
in a bowl and beat them until almost blended, adding a little ice water if the mixture
is too stiff. It is important that your butter is soft otherwise the mixture will curdle.

(CONTINUES ON NEXT PAGE)

(CONTINUED FROM PREVIOUS PAGE)

To make the royal icing, place the egg white in a bowl and, using a palette knife, blend in a little icing sugar at a time until the icing is a fairly thick consistency. Store the icing in a jar with a tight lid. Place about 3 tablespoons of icing in a piping bag with a small round nozzle.

To decorate the cupcakes, make up your colours by adding small amounts of colour gel to the sugar paste icing. Blend the colours in well by kneading the sugar paste. You can add colour gels to the royal icing as well, but just add a tiny bit at a time as they are very strong. Dust a clean work surface with cornflour (I find this works much better than icing sugar) and roll out the sugar-paste icing to about 3mm thick. Use round cookie cutters to cut out the shapes to cover the cupcakes. Place a small amount of butter icing on each cupcake, place the sugar-paste rounds over the butter icing and smooth it off with the ball of your hand. Repeat the procedure for all the other cupcakes.

To assemble the triple-tiered cupcakes, place the ready-decorated three different sizes on top of one another and, using the royal icing, pipe small balls around the bases of the top two cupcakes to secure them onto the bottom ones. Pipe small balls onto the sugar paste or tiny loops along the edges. (Don't make the loops too long as they will be too heavy and will drop off.) Finish off each triple cupcake by topping it with a sugar-paste rose.

Makes 10–12 triple cupcakes

orange and almond muffins

Classic, old-fashioned, not-too-sweet
muffins with just the right amount of almond.

250g butter, softened · 250g castor sugar
4 large eggs · 250g self-raising flour
zest of 2 oranges
I teaspoon almond essence (optional)
50g flaked almonds

Preheat the oven to 180°C. Line 18 muffin cups with baking paper squares.
Beat the softened butter and castor sugar together until light and fluffy.
Beat in the eggs one at a time. Fold in the flour and add
the zest and the almond essence. Spoon the mixture into the
muffin cups and sprinkle generously with flaked almonds.
Bake for 20 minutes, rotating the pans halfway through the baking time.

Makes 18

lemon and poppy seed cake

The prettiest guest at any tea table.

160ml yoghurt · 160ml vegetable oil · 300g castor sugar
300g self-raising flour · pinch of salt · 3 large eggs
50g poppy seeds · zest of 3 lemons
lemon-butter icing
1 quantity butter icing (see vanilla fairy cakes recipe) · zest of 1 lemon
sugar-paste icing
600g sugar-paste icing · 1 teaspoon tylose or cmc
(available from speciality baking stores)
yellow colouring gel · cornflour for dusting
royal icing
2 tablespoons royal icing (see vanilla fairy cakes recipe)

Preheat the oven to 180°C. Line three 10cm cake tins with baking paper.
Place the yoghurt, oil, castor sugar, self-raising flour, salt, eggs, poppy seeds
and zest of 3 lemons in a mixing bowl and beat for a few minutes until all the
ingredients are well combined. Split the mixture between the 3 tins and bake
for about 30 minutes or until a tester inserted into the cakes comes out clean,
rotating the tins halfway through the baking time. Allow the cakes to cool.

To make the lemon icing, follow the method for the butter icing
in the fairy cakes recipe, then mix in the zest of 1 lemon.

(CONTINUES ON NEXT PAGE)

(CONTINUED FROM PREVIOUS PAGE)

To assemble the cake, trim the tops of the cakes if necessary and
sandwich them together with lemon-butter icing. Then ice the cake
with a thin, smooth layer of lemon-butter icing. Dust a flat work surface
with cornflour and roll out 500g of white sugar-paste icing to about
3mm thick. Carefully lift the icing, drape it over the cake and then
smooth out all the folds until you have a smooth covering.
Trim the edges of the sugar-paste icing.

The sugar-paste flower decorations will need to be made at least
24 hours before you make the cake so they have time to harden.
To make them, mix a tiny bit of yellow colouring gel and the teaspoon of
tylose or cmc into the remaining 100g of sugar-paste icing and blend well.
Lightly dust a surface with cornflour, and roll out the icing to about ½mm.
Cut out tiny flowers in three different sizes. (Cutters are available from
speciality baking stores). Using tiny blobs of royal icing, attach the
flowers to the cake. Place the cake on a stand and finish it
off by piping little balls around its base.

Serves 6–8

dolly p's

Like their namesake, these are loud, rich and
slightly trashy looking — but loved just the same.

125g butter, softened · 165g castor sugar
1 teaspoon vanilla extract · 2 large eggs
185g flour · 1 teaspoon baking powder · 25g cocoa
125ml yoghurt · 2 teaspoons red colouring gel

1 quantity lemon cream cheese icing (see mini carrot cakes recipe)

Preheat the oven to 180°C. Line 12 muffin cups with 7cm cupcake holders.
In a mixing bowl, beat the butter, sugar and vanilla extract together
for 10 minutes until light and fluffy. Add the eggs one at a time, beating
between each addition. Add the rest of the ingredients and beat until
they are well combined. Spoon the mixture into the cupcake holders and
bake for 20 minutes, rotating the muffin pan halfway through the baking time.
Allow the cupcakes to cool and ice them with the lemon cream cheese icing.

Makes 10—12

passion-fruit cakes

The perfect marriage of light-as-air cake
and smooth, sweet passion-fruit curd.

60ml yoghurt · 60ml vegetable oil · 150g sugar · 150g self-raising flour
pinch of salt · 2 large eggs · 60ml passion-fruit pulp
passion-fruit curd
250g sugar · 100g butter · 60ml passion-fruit pulp · 3 large eggs
icing sugar for dusting

Preheat the oven to 180°C. Lightly grease two 10cm x 8cm heart-shaped
loose-bottomed cake tins. Place all the cake ingredients in a mixing bowl and
beat together for a few minutes until all the ingredients are well combined.
Divide the mixture between the tins and bake for 20 minutes, rotating
the tins halfway through the cooking time. Allow the cakes to cool.

To make the curd, place all the ingredients in the top of a double boiler
and heat, stirring, until all the ingredients have melted and combined.
Then allow the mixture to cook until it thickens, stirring occasionally.
The whole process takes about 45 minutes, so be sure to keep an eye
on the water levels in the double boiler and don't let it cook dry.

To assemble the cakes, sandwich the two layers together with the
passion-fruit curd. Dust the finished cakes lightly with icing sugar.

Serves 6—8

petits fours

So much easier to make than they look — the trick is
to freeze these before icing to prevent crumbling.

I quanity vanilla cupcake recipe (see vanilla fairy cakes recipe)
500g marzipan · apricot jam
fondant icing
6 large egg whites · 850g icing sugar

Preheat the oven to 180°C. Line a 22cm square cake tin with baking paper and wrap
the outside of the tin in foil so the cake cooks more evenly. Follow the method for the
vanilla fairy cakes, then pour the mixture into the tin and bake for about 50 minutes
or until a tester inserted comes out clean, turning the tin halfway through the baking
time. Allow the cake to cool completely before removing it from the tin.

Trim the top of the cake if necessary to make it flat. Spread a thin layer of
apricot jam over the top of the cake. Dust a surface with icing sugar and roll
out the marzipan to about 2mm thick. Lift it carefully and place it over the jam.
Trim the edges and then cut the cake into 4cm x 4cm squares (or smaller if you like).
Place them on a lined baking sheet and freeze them overnight or for up to a week.
This helps to avoid all the crumbs when you dip them into the fondant icing.

To make the fondant icing, place 3 egg whites in a bowl and slowly add 350g of icing
sugar until you have a thickish but still runny consistency. Take the petits fours out of
the freezer a few at a time and dip them in the icing, making sure they are completely
covered. Place them on a rack to dry. Then repeat the process with a thicker fondant
icing made by mixing the remaining 3 egg whites with 500g of icing sugar. Dip each
petit four in the icing and allow it to dry on the rack. Put each petit four into a mini
cupcake holder and decorate with frosted rose petals or tiny fondant flowers.

Makes 25

baked cheesecake

A sublime baked offering that doesn't skimp on the cream.

1 x 200g packet digestive biscuits
60g butter, melted · 900g cream cheese
3 large eggs · 200g castor sugar
3 tablespoons flour · 500g crème fraîche
1 teaspoon vanilla extract
500g fresh strawberries · icing sugar for dusting

Preheat the oven to 180°C. Crush the biscuits in a food processor and mix with the melted butter. Line the base of a 22cm spring-form tin with baking paper and place the biscuit mixture in the tin. Press into the tin with the back of a spoon and bake the base for 10 minutes. Place the cream cheese, eggs, sugar, flour, 250g of crème fraîche plus 2 extra tablespoons crème fraîche and vanilla extract in a bowl and mix together well. Pour into the baked base and bake for 15 minutes at 180°C, then turn the oven down to 140°C and bake for a further 50 minutes. Turn the oven off and allow the cheesecake to cool in the oven. (I usually bake it at night and then leave it in the oven till the next morning.) Refrigerate the cake for at least 1½ hours before you take it out of the tin. I have sometimes found that it gets a crack in the middle, in which case I just top it with an extra few tablespoons of crème fraîche, which finishes it off very well. Top with fresh hulled srawberries and dust generously with icing sugar.

Serves 8—10

55

meringues

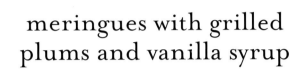

meringues with grilled plums and vanilla syrup

This is the best meringue recipe I have ever come across. You can use it to make any size of meringues, from tiny bites to luxurious dollops to pavlova bases. I even use this mixture for the top of my lemon meringue tart.

4 large egg whites · 225g castor sugar · 1 teaspoon cornflour
fresh thick or lightly whipped cream, to serve
grilled plums
8 plums, stoned and cut in half
4 tablespoons vanilla castor sugar · 4 tablespoons soft butter
vanilla syrup
400g castor sugar · 500ml water
1 vanilla pod, cut lengthways down the middle and scraped

Preheat the oven to 150°C. Line a baking tray with baking paper. To make the meringues, place the egg whites and sugar in the top of a double boiler and heat, stirring, until the mixture is just warm. Pour into a bowl and beat on high for 15 minutes until soft peaks form. Mix in the cornflour. Scoop 8 dollops of meringue onto the baking tray and bake for 1½ hours. Turn off the oven and allow the meringues to cool in the oven — this is what gives them gooey centres.

(CONTINUES ON NEXT PAGE)

(CONTINUED FROM PREVIOUS PAGE)

To make the grilled plums, line a baking tray and place the
plums on it, cut sides up. Sprinkle generously with vanilla castor
sugar and place a small knob of butter in the middle of each half plum.
Place under the grill for about 10 minutes or until a little charred,
but watch them carefully to ensure that they don't burn. (These plums
are also delicious on French toast, with lashings of crème fraîche.)

To make the vanilla syrup, place all the ingredients in a saucepan
or pot and simmer until they form a thickish clear syrup.

To serve, place a meringue on each plate, dollop with cream and
top with 2 grilled plum halves. Drizzle over the vanilla syrup.

Makes 8

chocolate and hazelnut meringue 'cupcakes'

Featuring the holy trinity of meringue appreciation — chocolate, nuts and cream.

100g toasted hazelnuts • 6 large egg whites • 350g castor sugar
1 teaspoon cornflour • 1 teaspoon white spirit vinegar
120g dark chocolate, melted

Preheat the oven to 180°C. Toast the hazelnuts in the oven for 20 minutes, then place them in a dishcloth and rub them vigorously to remove the skins. Chop them roughly. Reduce the oven temperature to 150°C, then prepare 12 muffin cups. To make the meringue, place the egg whites in a mixing bowl and beat them until they are fluffy. Add the sugar 1 tablespoon at a time, beating all the time. Mix in the cornflour and the vinegar and then beat for 12 minutes until the meringue mixture is fluffy and glossy. Half-fill the muffin cups with the meringue mixture, sprinkle a teaspoon of chopped toasted hazelnuts onto each one and top with another dollop of meringue mixture. Sprinkle the remaining nuts over the tops and bake for 1½ hours. These meringues rise quite a lot so make sure you have enough space above them. Switch off the oven and allow the meringues to cool in it. Once they have cooled completely, drizzle the melted chocolate over the meringues; they can be filled or served with whipped cream.

Makes 12

almond meringues with slow-roasted naartjies

Nuts always team brilliantly with meringues
and the naartjies add a citrusy twist.

1 quantity plain meringue
(see meringues with grilled plums and vanilla syrup recipe)
100g flaked almonds
8 naartjies, washed and cut in half
500ml freshly squeezed orange juice, strained
125ml golden syrup · 7 allspice berries · 100g white sugar

To make the meringues, follow the method for the meringues with
grilled plums and vanilla syrup recipe, scattering the meringues
with the flaked almonds before baking them.

To make the slow-roasted naartjies, preheat the oven to 180°C.
Place the naartjie halves in an oven dish, cut sides up, and pour the
orange juice over them. Drizzle with the golden syrup and scatter over
the allspice berries. Cover the tray with aluminium foil and roast the
naartjies for about 1½ hours. Remove the foil, sprinkle the sugar
over the naartjies and roast, uncovered, for a further ½ hour.
Allow the naartjies to cool.

To serve, place a meringue on each plate, top with two
naartjie halves and drizzle with the juices from the pan.

Makes 8

pistachio praline meringue discs

Use as the base for individual pavlovas, for cream-filled meringue sandwiches or as an accompaniment to a couple of ice cream scoops.

1 quantity plain meringue
(see meringues with grilled plums and vanilla syrup recipe)
pistachio praline
125ml sugar · 60ml water
100g shelled pistachio nuts

Follow the method for the plain meringue and make 10–12 flattish discs.

While they are cooking, make the pistachio praline. Shell the pistachios and place them on a baking tray lined with baking paper. Place the sugar and water in a saucepan and stir until the sugar has melted. Bring the mixture to a simmer and cook for about 5 minutes until it just starts to caramelize. Let it stand for a minute and then carefully pour it over the nuts. Allow the praline to cool and then roughly chop it with a sharp knife. Sprinkle the praline over the cooked meringue discs and serve with vanilla ice cream or dollops of whipped cream.

Makes 10–12

rose-water meringue cake

The ultimate blow-your-friends-away cake that's perfect
for tea parties, weddings and girlie get togethers.

12 large egg whites · 700g castor sugar
1½ teaspoons cornflour · 1½ teaspoons white spirit vinegar
2 teaspoons rose-water · 20 pink roses · 1 large egg white
100g castor sugar · 250ml cream, whipped

Preheat the oven to 150°C. Line the bottoms and sides of two 22cm spring-form cake tins with baking paper. To make the meringue, place the egg whites in a mixing bowl and beat them until they are fluffy. Add the sugar 1 tablespoon at a time, beating all the time. Mix in the cornflour, vinegar and rose-water and then beat for 12 minutes until the meringue mixture is fluffy and glossy. Split the mixture between the two tins and bake for 1½ hours. Turn off the oven and allow the meringue cakes to cool in it. Carefully remove them from the tins.

Remove the petals from 2 roses and dip them in the egg white, then in the castor sugar. Place them on a cooling rack to dry. Cut the stems of the remaining roses to about 6cm long. Dip each whole rose into the egg white, gently shake off any excess and then carefully roll the rose heads in the castor sugar. Place them on the rack to dry. To assemble the cake, sandwich the two meringues together with half the whipped cream. Top with the rest of the cream, carefully push the frosted roses into the top layer and sprinkle with the frosted rose petals.

Serves 10—12

lemon meringue tartlets

This is the most delicious pastry I have ever come across. It took me
two years to find and perfect the recipe and I call it my 'well-behaved
pastry' because that is exactly what it is — it doesn't shrink down the
sides of the tin and when you bake it blind you don't have to bother
with baking beans and paper. It is just the BEST!

well-behaved pastry
225g butter · 200g castor sugar · 2 large eggs · 500g flour
lemon filling
3 x 385g cans condensed milk · juice and zest of 3 lemons · 4 large egg yolks
meringue topping
8 large egg whites · 450g castor sugar

To make the pastry, combine the butter and sugar in a blender and while it
is still running, add the eggs, one at a time. Add the flour and blend until it
forms a dough. Refrigerate for at least 1 hour before using.

Preheat the oven to 180°C. Press the pastry into 20 tartlet tins (5cm–7cm diameter),
refrigerate for 30 minutes, and then bake blind for 10 minutes.

Meanwhile, make the lemon filling. Combine the condensed milk, lemon juice,
lemon zest and egg yolks in a bowl and mix until well combined. Spoon the lemon
mixture into the cooked tartlet shells and bake at 160°C for 20 minutes. Allow to cool.

To make the meringue topping, place the egg whites and the sugar in the top of
a double boiler and heat, stirring, until the mixture is just warm. Pour into a bowl and
beat on high for 12 minutes until soft peaks form. Scoop dollops of meringue onto the
top of the cooked lemon mixture and brown the top of the meringue on each tartlet
lightly with a kitchen blowtorch. (Every baker's kitchen should have one of these!)
This recipe can also be used to make one large 30cm tart.

Makes 20

chocolate and orange truffle meringue tarts

This sophisticated offering will certainly take
centre stage at any dinner party.

chocolate pastry
225g butter · 200g sugar · 3 large eggs · 450g flour · 50g cocoa
chocolate and orange truffle filling
300g dark chocolate · 150ml cream · zest of 1 orange
meringue topping
8 egg whites · 450g castor sugar

To make the pastry, combine the butter and sugar in a blender and while it is still
running, add the eggs one at a time. Add flour and cocoa and blend to form a dough.
Refrigerate for at least 1 hour before using. Press into 10–12 small 10cm x 5cm
greased rectangular tart tins and refrigerate again for 30 minutes. Preheat the oven
to 180°C and bake the pastry shells blind for 15 minutes. Allow to cool.

To make the truffle filling, place all the ingredients in the top of a double boiler
and heat gently until the chocolate has melted. Mix gently, set aside to cool slightly,
then pour into the cooled pastry shells. Place the tarts in the fridge overnight to allow
the truffle mixture to set completely before you remove them from the tart tins.

To make the meringue topping, place the egg whites and sugar in the top
of a double boiler and heat, stirring, until the mixture is just warm.
Pour into a bowl and beat on high for 12 minutes until soft peaks form.
Place the mixture in a piping bag with a 1cm piping nozzle, and pipe four little
pointed dollops onto each tart. Brown them with a kitchen blowtorch.

Makes 10–12

sweet tarts and pastries

german apple pies

A traditional sweet pie.

120g butter • 100g sugar • 1 egg • 1 teaspoon vanilla extract
250g flour • 1 teaspoon baking powder • pinch salt
8 apples, peeled, cored and sliced
cinnamon • 100g castor sugar

Make the pastry by creaming the butter and sugar together,
then add the egg and vanilla. Sift together the flour, baking powder
and salt and gradually add to the egg mixture. Knead into a ball,
wrap in clingfilm and refrigerate for 2 hours before using.

Preheat the oven to 180°C. Cook the apples in a little water for
5 minutes. Place them in 6 small bowls and sprinkle with cinnamon
and some castor sugar to taste. Break the pastry into walnut-sized
pieces and place on top of the apples. Sprinkle with castor
sugar and bake for 20 minutes until golden brown.

Makes 6

plum and marzipan tarts

These tarts are even better the day after you make them.

1 x 400g roll ready-made all-butter puff pastry
100g marzipan · 4 plums, stoned and thinly sliced
2 tablespoons castor sugar · 50g flaked almonds

Preheat the oven to 180°C. Open out the roll of pastry and cut it
into eight 5cm by 10cm rectangles. Place them on a lined baking sheet.
Thinly slice the marzipan and divide it between the eight rectangles.
Place half a thinly sliced plum on top of each marzipan-covered rectangle.
Sprinkle with the castor sugar and flaked almonds and bake for 20 minutes.

Makes 8

chocolate tarts

Just one is all you need to get your chocolate fix.

1 quantity well-behaved pastry (see lemon meringue tartlets recipe)
120g butter • 450g dark chocolate • 4 large eggs • 165g castor sugar
80ml cream • 1 teaspoon vanilla extract • 100g dark chocolate, melted

Preheat the oven to 180°C. Press the pastry into 18 greased
small (10cm diameter) tart tins and refrigerate for 20 minutes.
Bake the shells blind for 15 minutes, then allow to cool.

To make the chocolate filling, melt the butter and chocolate together in
a saucepan over a low heat. Beat the eggs, castor sugar, cream and vanilla extract
together until they are light and fluffy. Pour the butter-and-chocolate mixture
into the egg mixture, beating continuously, and continue to beat for 1 minute.
Pour into the cooled tart shells and bake for 15 minutes, turning all the tarts
around halfway through the baking time. Remove from the oven and
allow to cool completely before you remove them from the tart tins.

To make the chocolate shavings, melt 100g chocolate in a double boiler.
Pour it onto a metal or marble surface and allow it to set. Scrape a palette
knife along the chocolate to form curled chocolate shavings. To assemble
the tarts, top generously with chocolate shavings.

Makes 18

pecan nut tartlets

Chewy, gooey nut-studded rounds of deliciousness
— the honey makes all the difference.

1 quantity well-behaved pastry (see lemon meringue tartlets recipe)
85g butter · 50g honey · 50g castor sugar
200g pecan nuts · 150ml cream

Preheat the oven to 180°C. Press the pastry into 8 small
(6cm-diameter) greased tartlet tins and refrigerate for 20 minutes.
Bake the shells blind for 15 minutes, then allow to cool.

To make the filling, melt the butter, honey and sugar together in a pot.
Add the nuts and cream and allow the mixture to just start to bubble.
Spoon into the cooled tartlet shells and bake for 10–15 minutes, turning all
the tins around halfway through the baking time. Remove from the oven
and allow to cool completely before you remove them from the tins.

Makes 8

apple tarte tatin

This is a surprisingly easy and foolproof recipe
— serve with a healthy dollop of mascarpone.

400g castor sugar · 100ml water
4—6 apples, peeled, cored and halved · 2 tablespoons butter
1 roll ready-made puff pastry · mascarpone, to serve

Preheat the oven to 190°C. Place the sugar and water in a small
ovenproof pan and stir until combined. Turn the plate on and cook
until the sugar just starts to caramelize. Don't stir it while it is cooking
as it will crystallize if you do. Meanwhile, cook the apples in the butter
for 5 minutes. Once the sugar is ready, add the cooked apples to the
pan of caramel. Cover with puff pastry, tucking in the edges carefully,
and bake for 20 minutes. Allow the tart to cool slightly, loosen the
pastry around the edges and carefully flip it out of the pan, being
very careful not to burn yourself with the hot caramel.
Serve with dollops of mascarpone.

Serves 4—6

pear and almond tarts

This classic combination never goes out of fashion.

1 quantity well-behaved pastry (see lemon meringue tartlets recipe)
frangipane
125g butter, diced · 125g castor sugar
2 large eggs · 100g ground almonds
4 pears, halved, cored and sliced · flaked almonds, to serve

Preheat the oven to 180°C. Press the pastry into 8–10 greased
small (10cm x 5cm diameter) tart tins and refrigerate for 30 minutes.
Bake the shells blind for 10 minutes, then allow to cool.

To make the frangipane, mix the butter and castor sugar in a food processor.
Add the eggs, one at a time, while the motor is still running and then
add the ground almonds and blend well. Place a dollop of frangipane
in each cooled tart shell and place 3 pear slices on top of each one.
Sprinkle with flaked almonds and bake for 35 minutes, turning all
the tarts around halfway through the baking time.

Makes 8–10

luxurious fruit mince pies

A year-round treat — the almond frangipane ensures it is not too heavy.

1 quantity well-behaved pastry (see lemon meringue tartlets recipe)
fruit mince
500g sultanas · 180g currants · 200g raisins · 125g dried dates, stoned
125g prunes, stoned · 125g glace cherries, chopped · 125g dried apricots
60g glacé ginger · 60g mixed peel · 2 apples, peeled, cored and grated
80ml fig jam · zest of 2 oranges · 2 tablespoons lemon juice
225g brown treacle sugar · 2 teaspoons ground allspice · 150ml brandy
1 portion frangipane (see pear and almond tarts recipe)
100g flaked almonds

Mix all the ingredients for the fruit mince together in a large bowl, cover with
clingwrap and store in the fridge for 1 month, stirring it every 2–3 days. If you
don't want to make your own, use a good quality store-bought fruit mince.

Preheat the oven to 180°C. Press the pastry into 24 small (mince pie-sized)
tart tins and refrigerate for 30 minutes. Bake the pastry shells blind for
10 minutes, then allow to cool. Place a teaspoon of fruit mince in each shell,
top with a teaspoon of frangipane and sprinkle with flaked almonds.
Bake for 15–20 minutes and allow to cool before removing from the tins.

Makes 24

lemon tartlets

Not too sharp and not too sweet and perfectly bite-sized too.

1 quantity well-behaved pastry (see lemon meringue tartlets recipe)
lemon filling
6 lemons · 5 large egg yolks
160g castor sugar, plus extra for dusting · 150ml crème fraîche

Preheat the oven to 180°C. Press the pastry into 40 greased
very small tart tins and refrigerate for 30 minutes. Bake the
shells blind for 10 minutes, then allow to cool.

Reduce the oven temperature to 120°C. To make the lemon filling,
finely grate the rind of 3 lemons and add the juice of all six. Beat the egg
yolks and castor sugar together well and then add the lemon juice and zest.
Blend them well and then add the crème fraîche. Allow the mixture to
stand for at least 1 hour and skim the froth off the top before you pour
it into the cooled tart shells. Carefully fill the shells and bake for about
30 minutes. They will still be wobbly when they come out of the oven but
will set as they cool. (The low cooking temperature prevents the lemon
mixture from cracking.) Dust the cooled tarts with castor sugar and
caramelize the sugar with a kitchen blowtorch.

Makes 40

plum and apple pie

An old-fashioned kind of pie with a lovely flaky pastry crust.

250g flour, plus extra for rolling
1 tablespoon castor sugar, plus extra for dusting
¼ teaspoon baking powder · 180g butter
80ml ice-cold water · 1 teaspoon vanilla extract
6 apples, peeled, cut in half and cored
6 plums, stoned and cut in half
crème fraîche or whipped fresh cream, to serve

Place the flour, castor sugar, baking powder and butter in a food
processor and combine well. While the motor is running, add the cold
water and vanilla extract and continue to process until it forms
a smooth dough. Wrap in clingwrap and refrigerate for 30 minutes.
(This pastry can also be made the day before.)

Preheat the oven to 180°C. Place the fruit in an oven dish.
Lightly dust a clean flat surface with flour and roll the pastry out to about
3mm thick. Carefully lift the pastry, place over the dish to cover the fruit
and trim the edges. Dust with castor sugar and bake for 30–35 minutes.
Serve with generous dollops of crème fraîche or whipped cream.

Serves 6–8

chocolate and almond phyllo rolls

So impressive and yet so easy to make
— freeze these unbaked for impromptu puddings.

170g dark chocolate, roughly chopped · 80ml cream
¼ teaspoon ground cinnamon · 150g toasted almonds, roughly chopped
3 sheets phyllo pastry · 100g butter, melted · icing sugar for dusting

Place the chocolate in a bowl. Heat the cream with the
cinnamon until just simmering and pour it over the chocolate.
Stir until the chocolate has melted. Finely chop 2 tablespoons of
nuts and set them aside. Stir the rest of the nuts into the chocolate.
Preheat the oven to 180°C. Place the chocolate mixture in a plastic bag and
allow it to cool. Cut a 2cm hole in the corner of the bag. Place a sheet of
phyllo pastry on a flat surface and brush with melted butter, then place
another one on top and brush with more butter. Repeat with a third sheet.
Pipe the chocolate mixture along the short side of the pastry, about
5cm in from the edges. Tuck in the ends and roll it into a tight log.
Seal the ends by brushing them with a little melted butter.
Place the log on a lined baking sheet and bake for 15 minutes.
Remove from the oven, brush the log with butter and sprinkle
the 2 tablespoons of nuts over the log. Rotate the tray when replacing
it in the oven to bake for another 15 minutes. Allow the log to cool
and then cut it diagonally into 6 portions.

Serves 6

apricot custard tart

For the not-so-sweet-toothed — be sure to eat it on the day it's made.

1 quantity well-behaved pastry (see lemon meringue tartlets recipe)
125ml thick cream · 1 large egg · 2 teaspoons castor sugar
30g butter, melted · 18–20 apricots, stoned and cut in half
whipped fresh cream, to serve

Preheat the oven to 180°C. Press the pastry into a 30cm x 12cm
rectangular tart dish and refrigerate for 30 minutes. Bake the pastry
shell blind for 15 minutes. Increase the oven temperature to 220°C.
Meanwhile, beat the cream and egg together and then beat in the
castor sugar. Pour the melted butter into the cream mixture and mix.
Place the pastry shell on a baking sheet and layer the apricot halves
in the pastry shell, cut sides up. Carefully pour the custard into
the shell over the apricots and bake for 25–30 minutes.
Serve with generous dollops of whipped fresh cream.

Serves 6–8

savoury tarts and old-fashioned pies

balsamic onion and olive tarts

The sweet caramelized onions and salty
olives are the perfect dance partners.

1 x 400g roll ready-made all-butter puff pastry • flour for dusting
about 24 kalamata olives, stones removed
balsamic onions
8 medium onions, peeled and quartered
125ml brown treacle sugar • 250ml balsamic vinegar
cream filling
325ml fresh cream • 2 large eggs • salt and freshly ground pepper

Preheat the oven to 180˚C. Prepare the pastry shells by rolling out the
puff pastry and cutting out six 12cm rounds. Line six lightly greased
10cm tart tins with pastry and place them in the fridge to rest.

Meanwhile, make the balsamic onions. Place all the ingredients in a pan
and cook them very gently for about 45 minutes, stirring occasionally until
the onions have softened and the balsamic vinegar has reduced. Fill the tart shells
with the balsamic onions and place about 4 stoned kalamata olives on each tart.
Combine the ingredients for the cream mixture and carefully fill the tarts.
Bake them for about 50 minutes, turning all the tins halfway through the baking time.
If you want to make a large tart, bake it for about 1 hour until golden brown.

Makes 6

caramelized onion and bacon tart

Make this in trays and serve for brunch
— or as a round tart for a sophisticated lunch.

3 tablespoons vegetable oil · 12 medium onions, peeled
and thinly sliced · 8 slices streaky bacon · 1 quantity cream filling
(see balsamic onion and olive tarts recipe)

pastry
250g flour, plus extra for dusting · 120g butter
100g cream cheese · 3 tablespoons cold water

To make the pastry, place the flour and butter in a food processor
and blend until just combined. Add the cream cheese and water and pulse
until blended. Roll into a ball, wrap the pastry in clingfilm and refrigerate for
at least 1 hour. Preheat the oven to 180°C. Lightly dust a work surface and roll
out the pastry to about 2mm thick. Carefully lift the pastry and line a lightly
greased 22cm loose-bottomed tart tin. Press the pastry into the corners and
refrigerate for 30 minutes. Bake the shell blind for 25—30 minutes.

To make the filling, gently fry the onions in the oil, stirring occasionally,
until they are golden brown. (It will take about 45 minutes.) Spoon the
onions into the tart shell. Cut the bacon into small pieces and dot them over
the onions. Carefully pour the cream filling into the tart shell and bake
for about 50 minutes until golden brown. If you make a larger tart,
you will need to cook it for a slightly longer time.

Serves 6—8

baby tomato, feta and bacon tarts with cheese pastry

Served with a crisp salad, this is a foolproof crowd-pleaser.

18 baby rosa tomatoes, halved
3 slices streaky bacon · 100g Danish feta
1 quantity cream filling (see balsamic onion and olive tarts recipe)
cheese pastry
100g flour · 100g butter · 100g cheddar, grated

To make the pastry, place all the ingredients in a food processor until they are combined and form a ball. If it is a little sticky, add a bit more flour. Wrap the pastry in clingwrap and refrigerate for 1 hour. Press the pastry into six 10cm x 5cm loose-bottomed tart tins and refrigerate for 1 hour.

Preheat the oven to 180°C. Place 6 tomato halves in each tart shell, split the feta between the six tarts and place half a slice of streaky bacon on the top of each tart. Carefully pour the cream filling into each tart shell and bake for about 40 minutes until golden brown.

Makes 6

leek and goat's cheese phyllo parcels

A sophisticated savoury bake that's so easy to prepare.

6 large leeks, washed and sliced · 3 tablespoons olive oil
salt and pepper · 100g goat's cheese
3 sheets phyllo pastry · 100g butter, melted
1 quantity cream filling (see balsamic onion and olive tarts recipe)

Preheat the oven to 180°C. Fry the leeks in the olive oil until just golden
and season with salt and pepper. Place the three sheets of phyllo pastry
on top of each other and cut them into 12cm x 12cm squares. Lightly grease
a 12-cup muffin tin. Brush each pastry square with the melted butter and place
three squares in each muffin cup. Fill the parcels with leeks and split the goat's
cheese evenly between them. Carefully fill with the cream filling and bake for
45 minutes until the pastry is golden brown and the filling is firm and cooked
through. Allow the parcels to cool and carefully remove them from the tins.

Makes 12

wild mushroom and pecorino tart

A virtually instant tart complete with
wonky edges and robust flavours.

1 x 400g roll ready-made all-butter puff pastry · flour for dusting
50g grated pecorino · 300g mix of shiitake and porcini mushrooms
4 tablespoons olive oil, plus extra for drizzling · salt and pepper
50g pecorino shavings · 50g rocket

Preheat the oven to 180°C. Place the pastry on a lightly floured surface and
sprinkle with the grated pecorino. Fold the pastry in half and give it two rolls,
fold in half again and give it another two rolls. Cut out a rough 20cm circle
and place it on a baking sheet lined with baking paper. Place it in the fridge
to rest until you are ready to use it. Fry the mushrooms in the olive oil and
season with salt and pepper. Place the mushrooms on top of the pastry and
bake for 30 minutes until the pastry puffs up and turns golden brown. To serve,
top with the pecorino shavings and rocket, and drizzle with a little extra olive oil.

Serves 6—8

lamb and baby onion pie

A rib-sticking winter choice made with
lamb knuckles and whole baby onions.

1kg lamb knuckles · 4 tablespoons olive oil · 125ml red wine
500g baby onions, peeled · 1.5 litres beef or chicken stock
4 bay leaves · 1 tablespoon freshly ground pepper
4 carrots, peeled and sliced diagonally · salt
1 x 400g roll ready-made all-butter puff pastry
1 slice onion · 1 large egg, beaten

Fry the knuckles in the olive oil until browned, adding a little of the red wine
at a time. Add the baby onions and continue frying for about 5 minutes.
Add 750ml of stock, the bay leaves and the black pepper and simmer gently
for about 1½ hours or until the lamb starts to fall off the bone, topping up the
stock levels as it simmers until all the stock has been added. Add the carrots and
simmer for a further 30 minutes. Allow the lamb to stand for a few hours before
using it to allow the flavours to develop. Season with salt. Preheat the oven to 180°C.
Place the lamb mixture in a pie dish and cover with the pastry, trimming the edges.
Place the onion slice in the middle of the pastry and brush the top of the
pie with the beaten egg. Bake for 25 minutes until golden brown.

Serves 4

butternut and sage triangles

Make a double batch of these crowd pleasers and
freeze them for those impromptu drinks get-togethers.

300g butternut, peeled and diced • 200g butter
24 sage leaves • salt and pepper • 4 sheets phyllo pastry

Preheat the oven to 180°C.
Steam the butternut and mash it roughly with a fork.
Melt the butter in a pan, add the sage leaves and simmer gently
until the leaves are just crisp. (Take care that the butter doesn't burn.)
Pour half the butter into the butternut and add half the sage leaves.
Blend them well, breaking up the crispy leaves. Season with salt and pepper.
Place a sheet of phyllo pastry on a flat surface and brush generously
with the remaining sage butter. Cut each sheet into four long strips.
Place a teaspoon of the butternut mixture in the corner of one strip and
fold the corner into a triangle. Continue folding the pastry into a triangle
shape, brushing it with the butter as you fold. As you get to the last fold,
place a sage leaf on the pastry, do the final fold covering the leaf
and seal the triangle with more sage butter. Repeat the process
for all the others. Place the triangles on baking tray and
bake for 20–25 minutes until golden brown.

Makes 12

baby tomato tarte tatin

It's the splash of balsamic reduction that brings out
all the summery flavour in this savoury offering.

350g baby tomatoes · 1 tablespoon olive oil
salt and pepper · 1 teaspoon sugar
1 tablespoon balsamic reduction (available from speciality food stores)
1 x 400g roll ready-made all-butter puff pastry

Preheat the oven to 180°C. In an oven-proof pan, flash-fry the baby
tomatoes in the olive oil for 1 minute and then add the salt and pepper,
sugar and balsamic reduction. Roll out the puff pastry and cut out
a circle to fit the pan. Place the pastry over the tomatoes and tuck
the edges in around them. Bake for 20–25 minutes until the pastry
puffs up and turns golden. Take it out of the oven and allow it to
cool for 10 minutes. Run a knife around the edges to loosen
the pastry and then carefully flip the tart onto a plate.

Serves 2–3

creamy spinach and fish pie

The ultimate no-fuss comfort-food offering
— the fish cooks in the creamy spinach sauce.

1kg spinach, washed, stalks removed and chopped
2 cloves garlic, crushed · 2 tablespoons olive oil · 500ml fresh cream
800g white fish (kabejou or hake), cut into bite-sized pieces
5 potatoes, peeled · 3 tablespoons butter · 80ml fresh cream
salt and pepper · 2 tablespoons olive oil

Preheat the oven to 180°C. Steam the spinach
until it has just wilted, drain it and allow it to cool.
Squeeze out any excess water. Fry the garlic in the olive oil
for a minute, then add the spinach and fry for a few minutes.
Add the 500ml cream and simmer gently for 5 minutes.
Add the raw fish and mix. Place the mixture in an oven-proof
dish. To make the topping, cook the potatoes until soft, mash
them well and push them through a sieve. Add the cream and
1 tablespoon of the butter and season well with salt and pepper.
Cover the top of the spinach and fish mixture with the mash,
dot the remaining butter over the top and drizzle with the olive oil.
Bake for 30 minutes until the mash is golden brown.

Serves 8

homemade chicken and mushroom pies

Quintessential old-fashioned chicken pies with puff-pastry topping.

2 roast chickens · 2 x 400g rolls ready-made all-butter puff pastry
2 onions, thinly sliced · 3 tablespoons olive oil
250g brown mushrooms, roughly chopped
750ml fresh cream · 2 tablespoons flour · salt and pepper
1 large egg · 2 tablespoons milk

Preheat the oven to 180˚C. Remove all the flesh from
the roast chickens and set the bones and skin aside.
(You can make a tasty stock with them.) Fry the onions in the oil
until golden brown, then add the chicken and mushrooms.
Stir them together and cook for a few minutes.
Add the cream and the flour and cook until the cream
thickens, but watch that it doesn't catch on the bottom of
the pot. Season with salt and a good grind of black pepper.
Fill 8–10 ramekins with the chicken mixture and top with
a round of puff pastry. Cut out letters using tiny alphabet
cutters and place them on top of the pie. Prick three
holes in the top of the pasty. Mix the egg and milk
together and brush over the pastry using a pastry brush.
Bake for 20–25 minutes until golden brown.

Makes 8–10

fig and gorgonzola tarts

It'd be a sin not to make this in fig season
— serve with a glass of bubbly.

2 x 400g rolls ready-made all-butter puff pastry
200g gorgonzola · 16 fresh figs, halved · 16 rocket leaves
balsamic reduction (available from speciality food stores)
black pepper

Preheat the oven to 180°C. Unroll the pastry and cut each roll
into 4 rectangles. Place the pastry pieces on a baking sheet lined
with baking paper. Cover them with another piece of baking
paper and place another baking sheet on top so it flattens them.
Bake the pastry for 20–25 minutes until crisp. (You can cut them
smaller and use them for the bases of other tasty fillings.) Split the
gorgonzola between the 8 bases and top each base with 4 fig halves.
Bake for 8–10 minutes until the cheese just starts to bubble.
Top with fresh rocket, drizzle with balsamic reduction
and sprinkle over a good grind of black pepper.

Makes 8

salmon wellingtons

These take five minutes to make and are
the perfect mid-week summer supper.

2 x 400g rolls ready-made all-butter puff pastry
4 100g salmon fillets · 2 tablespoons basil pesto
2 tablespoons lemon juice · 1 large egg, beaten
1 teaspoon poppy seeds · salt and pepper
1 lemon, cut into wedges, to serve

Preheat the oven to 200°C. Unroll and cut one roll of pastry in half
and then in half again. Place 1 salmon fillet on each piece of pastry.
Mix the pesto and lemon juice together and spread over the fish. Season
with salt and pepper. Unroll and cut the other roll of pastry into quarters,
and lay each of the 4 resulting pastry pieces over the fillets. Cut slits down
the length of each one, separating the slits slightly. Pinch the sides of
the pastry together and trim to make neat rectangles. Brush the pastries
with the beaten egg and sprinkle with poppy seeds. Carefully place the
parcels on a lined baking tray and bake for 20–25 minutes at 200°C.
Serve with lemon wedges for squeezing over the fish.

Makes 4

breads and buns

scones

Perfectly light and fluffy 10-minute scones.

500g self-raising flour · 1 teaspoon baking powder
1 tablespoon castor sugar · ½ teaspoon salt · 60g butter, diced
1 large egg, beaten · 250ml buttermilk · milk for glazing

Preheat the oven to 200°C. Sift the flour and baking powder together
in a bowl. Stir in the sugar and salt and then add the diced butter.
Rub the butter into the flour using your fingertips until it looks like
breadcrumbs. Add the egg to the buttermilk and beat, then add this
mixture to the flour. Mix together, gather into a ball and knead lightly.
Flatten to about 3cm thick and cut out rounds with a cookie cutter.
Place them on a lined baking tray, brush with milk and bake
for 10–12 minutes or until golden brown and risen.

Makes 15

mom's buttermilk bread

The lazy baker's bread — throw it all
together and let the oven do the work.

450g nutty wheat flour · 2 tablespoons milk powder
1 tablespoon honey · 1 teaspoon salt
1 teaspoon bicarbonate of soda · 500ml buttermilk
½ teaspoon sunflower seeds
½ teaspoon poppy seeds · ½ teaspoon linseeds

Preheat the oven to 180°C. Place all the ingredients except
the seeds in a mixing bowl and mix to a sticky dough. Spoon into
a loaf tin lined with baking paper. Sprinkle with the seeds and bake
for 1¼ hours until golden brown. Tap the bottom of the tin to
test if it's done — the loaf should have a hollow sound.

Makes 1 loaf

seed loaf

A hearty and wholesome bread that
makes excellent toast and sandwiches.

2 tablespoons honey · 10g dried yeast · 600ml warm water
350g nutty wheat · 160g oats · 150g crushed wheat
75g poppy seeds, reserve ½ teaspoon
150g sunflower seeds, reserve ½ teaspoon
1 tablespoon sunflower oil · 2 teaspoons salt

Place the honey, yeast and 100ml of the warm water in a bowl and set
it aside to rise in a warm spot for 5 minutes. Mix the rest of the ingredients
together with the remaining 500ml of warm water. Add the yeast mixture and
blend together well. Spoon the mixture into a loaf tin lined with baking
paper, sprinkle with the reserved seeds and allow it to rise for 20 minutes.
Meanwhile, preheat the oven to 200°C. Bake for about 1 hour. Tap the bottom
of the tin to test if it's done — the loaf should have a hollow sound.

Makes 1 loaf

country buns

Smear these classic white buns with butter
and sandwich with thick wedges of cheese.

500g flour · 1 teaspoon salt
10g dried yeast · 300ml warm water
1 tablespoon olive oil

Sift the flour and salt into a large mixing bowl and stir in the yeast.
Make a well in the centre and gradually add the warm water and the olive oil.
Tip out the dough onto a lightly floured surface and knead for 10 minutes
until it is smooth. Shape it into 6 buns (or 1 loaf) and place on a lined
baking sheet. Cover with a tea towel and allow to rise for 25 minutes until
doubled in size. Meanwhile, preheat the oven to 220°C. Make diagonal
cuts in the top of the dough and bake for 20–25 minutes. If making
a loaf, place the kneaded dough in a loaf tin and allow it to rise for
25 minutes before baking for 35–40 minutes.

Makes 6 buns or 1 loaf

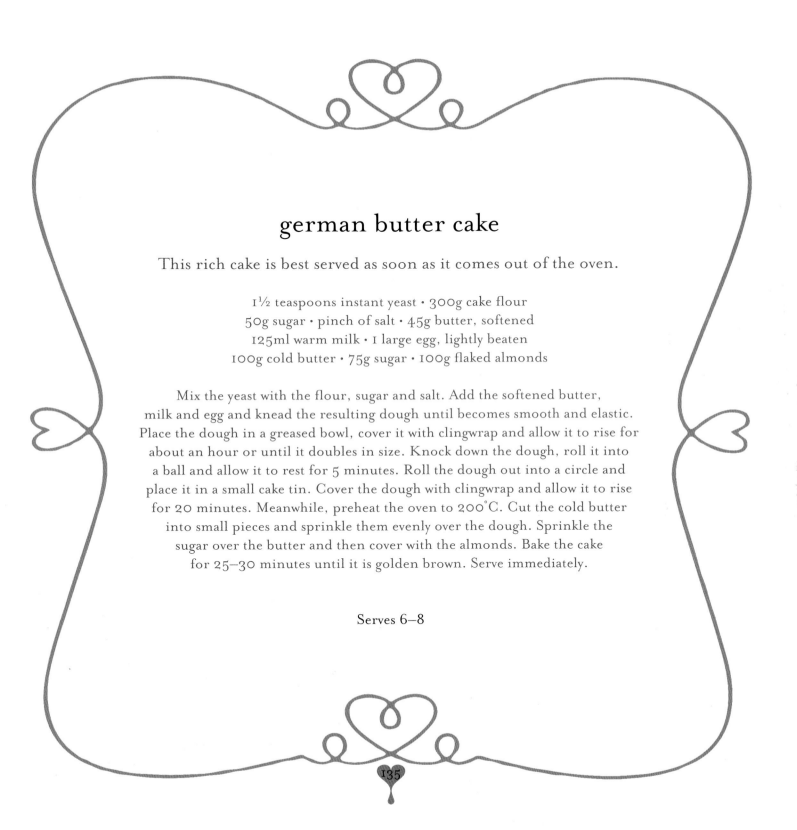

german butter cake

This rich cake is best served as soon as it comes out of the oven.

1½ teaspoons instant yeast • 300g cake flour
50g sugar • pinch of salt • 45g butter, softened
125ml warm milk • 1 large egg, lightly beaten
100g cold butter • 75g sugar • 100g flaked almonds

Mix the yeast with the flour, sugar and salt. Add the softened butter,
milk and egg and knead the resulting dough until becomes smooth and elastic.
Place the dough in a greased bowl, cover it with clingwrap and allow it to rise for
about an hour or until it doubles in size. Knock down the dough, roll it into
a ball and allow it to rest for 5 minutes. Roll the dough out into a circle and
place it in a small cake tin. Cover the dough with clingwrap and allow it to rise
for 20 minutes. Meanwhile, preheat the oven to 200°C. Cut the cold butter
into small pieces and sprinkle them evenly over the dough. Sprinkle the
sugar over the butter and then cover with the almonds. Bake the cake
for 25–30 minutes until it is golden brown. Serve immediately.

Serves 6–8

Lunch

• Savoury tart + salad 45
• Grilled aubergine, feta,
pesto, red pepper +
fresh tomato S/W 48
or salad 58
• Crispy bacon, balsamic
honey chicken +
camembert S/W 48
or salad 58
• Thai ginger chicken
curry + basmati rice 58
• Penne with tomato,
rocket + pecorino +
pesto 58
HOMEMADE CHICKEN
MUSHROOM PIE R60
with bu... 27...+ salad

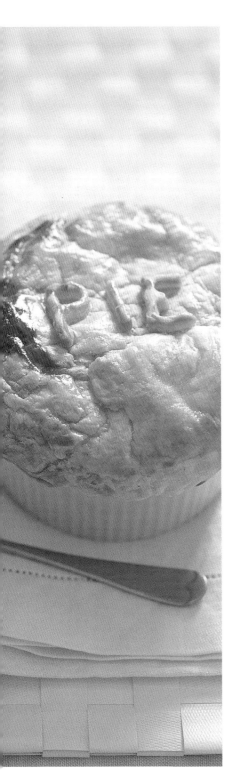

conversion table

MEASUREMENTS

STANDARD	METRIC
1/4 inch	5mm
1/2 inch	1cm
1 inch	2,5cm
2 inches	5cm
3 inches	7cm
4 inches	10cm
5 inches	12cm
6 inches	15cm
7 inches	18cm
8 inches	20cm
9 inches	23cm
10 inches	25cm
11 inches	28cm
12 inches	30cm

LIQUID MEASURE

STANDARD	METRIC
1 teaspoon	5ml
1 tablespoon	15ml
1 desertspoon	2 teaspoons
1/4 cup	60ml
1/3 cup	80ml
1/2 cup	125ml
2/3 cup	160ml
3/4 cup	175ml
3/4 cup	180ml
1 cup	250ml
1 1/4 cups	300ml
1 1/2 cups	375ml
1 2/3 cups	400ml
1 3/4 cups	450ml
2 cups	500ml
2 1/2 cups	600ml
3 cups	750ml

WEIGHT

STANDARD	METRIC
1/2 oz	15g
1 oz	30g
2 oz	60g
3 oz	90g
4 oz	125g
6 oz	175g
8 oz	250g
10 oz	300g
12 oz	375g
13 oz	400g
14 oz	425g
1 lb	500g
11/2lb	750g
2 lb	1 kg

OVEN TEMPERATURE

FAHRENHEIT	CELSIUS	DESCRIPTION
225°F	110°C	Cool
250°F	120°C	Cool
275°F	140°C	Very slow
300°F	150°C	Very slow
325°F	160°C	Slow
350°F	180°C	Moderate
375°F	190°C	Moderate
400°F	200°C	Moderately Hot
425°F	220°C	Hot
450°F	230°C	Hot

cook's notes

I am hoping that this book has made all those potential
bakers out there a little less fearful. I have to confess that before
I opened my restaurant, Queen of Tarts, I didn't bake, but it's been
an exciting and tasty journey getting to this point. Just a few
pointers, most of them obvious, that I have learnt over the years:

No two ovens are the same. The baking times in this book are
a suggestion. I always set my buzzer for slightly less time just to make
sure I don't overcook anything. I believe in using the good stuff in my
kitchen, and that means dollops of farm butter, lashings of fresh cream
(don't even think about substituting it for milk) and lots of other fresh tasty
ingredients. It's also always better to use castor sugar as opposed to
the coarser version, it makes for finer cakes — and always remember
to put it through a sieve to avoid any sugar lumps. One of my favourite
pastimes is making meringues. I love the glossy beaten egg whites and the best
investment I have made when it comes to meringues is buying a kitchen blowtorch. It adds a professional look to tart toppings and it's great fun to use.
And lastly, all the pastries and the frangipane in the book can be
frozen, so don't throw away any leftovers. Just wrap them up,
label them and pop them in the freezer.

Enjoy baking!
Tina Bester

TO MY EXTRAORDINARY DAUGHTER, ALI

thanks

A special, special, thanks…

To my mom, who has tirelessly listened to all my shop tales and who gives me all the love and support I need. To my brother Rory, you are fantastic! To Ali, my beautiful daughter, who makes me laugh. To Gran, for all your support over the years. To my niece Maya, for all your help on our first day of photography. To Pat Fraser, RIP, for your delicious shortbread recipe. To Carol for being the most rock-solid friend I could ever ask for. To Keri for divulging your chocolate cupcake recipe, it is legendary. To Rory for your love and encouragement, you are such a delight. To Craig and Libby and the Quivertree team for putting a spectacular book together, you are an amazing team. To Vicky for your gorgeous words and to Robyn for your meticulous editing. To Fred Swart for your unbelievable design of the Queen of Tarts logo, it has been much admired over the years. To Mdu, for your superb barista expertise and charming way with the customers and to all my queens in the shop, Asanda, Siti, Nono, Connie and Odi, I would not be able to do this without you. You are all such great women!

RECIPES TINA BESTER **WORDS** VICKI SLEET **PHOTOGRAPHS** CRAIG FRASER
DESIGN & PRODUCTION LIBBY DOYLE **DTP** BRIDGITTE CHEMALY
COPY EDITOR ROBYN ALEXANDER **SCANNING** RAY'S PHOTO CONTROL

QUEEN OF TARTS LOGO DESIGN FRED SWART, STUDIO STAMP 082-341-2819
PROPS SUE LANGEMAN 0721861403 HOUSE AND INTERIORS (021) 6831468 BIGGIE BEST (021) 6741590

FIRST PUBLISHED IN 2009 BY QUIVERTREE PUBLICATIONS
PO Box 51051 · Waterfront · 8002 · Cape Town · South Africa
T: +27 (0) 21 461 6808 · F: +27 (0) 21 461 6842 · E: info@quivertree.co.za
www.quivertreepublications.com · www.quivertreeimages.com

THIS EDITION PUBLISHED IN 2010 BY PAVILION,
AN IMPRINT OF THE ANOVA BOOKS GROUP LIMITED,
10, SOUTHCOMBE STREET, LONDON, W14 0RA